Clean Margins

Clean Margins

Poems by

Karen Steiger

© 2025 Karen Steiger. All rights reserved.
This material may not be reproduced in any form, published,
reprinted, recorded, performed, broadcast,
rewritten, or redistributed without
the explicit permission of Karen Steiger.
All such actions are strictly prohibited by law.

Cover design by Shay Culligan
Cover image by Stress Fibers and Microtubules in
Human Breast Cancer Cells. Created by Christina Stuelten
Carole Parent, 2011. The National Cancer Institute.
Author Photo by Jakub Ginda, GP Looks

ISBN: 978-1-63980-898-4

Kelsay Books
502 South 1040 East, A-119
American Fork, Utah 84003
Kelsaybooks.com

"As you know cancer is a burdensome disease.
I don't recommend it for anyone."

—My father, Norman, in a letter to his brother, Richard
July 14, 1982

Acknowledgments

Bombfire Lit: "My Ongoing Dispute with My Long-Term Disability Carrier," "Toxicity"
Crow and Cross Keys: "A Bit of a Meltdown"
Journal of Erato: "Tarot Reading"
The Midlife Crisis Poet: "Oceanic," "Bad News Sonnet," "Encounter with a Possum on an Evening Walk," "Stasis," "The Olympian Flu," "Tumbling," "Follow Up," "Cerebellum," "Luna"
Mineral Lit Mag: "The First of the Plagues"
Pendemic: "Stasis"
Perhappened: "Cotton Candy, 1983"
Sledgehammer Lit: "First, the Rules," "Mastectomy"
Tales from the Trail: "The Eternal"
Twist in Time: "bean sí"

To fully thank everyone in my life would require more pages than all the poetry I've ever written, but I'd like to begin of course, with my mom, Mary Ann Steiger; my brother, David; and my cousins, Rick Macchia, Dawn Tornusciolo, and Chrissy Swafford. I'd also like to thank the Allison Family, especially Earl; Steve and Amy; Kennedy; Wendy and Steve; and Kathy. My love goes out to Zeborah Allison, C.J. Terrell, and Damon Etawlyah.

I think just about every medical professional in Elk Grove Village, IL, saw or poked at my breasts during the period of 2019–2021, and I owe so much to them for saving my life and restoring me back to my normal crazy self, especially Dr. Jerry Andrews; Dr. Steven Kanter; Yanina Zborovskaya, DNP; Dr. James M. Kane, Jr.; Dr. Ramji Rajendran; Dr. Stephen Madry; Claire Gates; Christie Downing; and any other techs, nurses, and medical staff on the case.

I am of course indebted to the members of the Schaumburg Poetry Group and St. Mary's Episcopal Church in Park Ridge. A special thank you to everyone at Gilda's Club. As Gilda Radner once said, it's a club no one wants to join, but if you are at all impacted by cancer, it is an incredible organization that I can't recommend enough.

I would like to thank my employers at I/O Solutions, who had every right to fire me after my FMLA leave was up but who allowed me to keep my health insurance when I had multiple surgeries and radiation ahead. The American health care system is really messed up.

My eternal gratitude to Ankh Spice, Kristi Weber, and Leanna House for their kind words in support of this book. I am so thrilled to work with Laura Berry and Arin Ciulla on my merch! Thanks to Martin Atkins for inspiring me to market this book creatively.

Thank you to Karen Kelsay, Olivia Loftis, and Jenna Wray and everyone at Kelsay Books for saying yes when so many people said no.

To name my dear friends puts me at the risk of accidentally leaving someone out, but I'd like to thank the following individuals (in no particular order!) for their care, concern, and love: Amanda and Mike Hayes; Padraig Johnston and Matt Weiler; Monica Johnston; Laura and Shawn Berry; Roy Rummelhart; Lindsey Bresee; Samantha Romano and Jason Lundsgaard; Samuel Romano; Gina and Bob Ciulla; Marita McQuaid; Jennifer and Dave Wilcoxson; Jeanette Jaskula and Mike Nichols; Louise Tylman; Annie and Jeff Miller; Aaron Houston; Nancy Marszalek and Eric Ostrander; Melissa, Travis, Annabelle, and Colton Kramer; Amanda Dickson; Jesse and Rachel Olson; Rita Chodor; Elisse Lorenc; Emily

Patterson-Kane; Susan Swanson; Steve and Afua Kim; the entire Burnside Family (my adopted family in California): Dan, Jaime, Huxley, and Shelley Layne; Bryan and Miranda Bishop; Jaime Lilley; Naomi Beck-Mesbur; Courtney Sanger; Amber Handelman; Erin Best; Megan Brennan; Annie Roca; Catalina Salley; Becky Elliott-Kotsinis; Meghan Kooi; Chris Fisher; Elissa Bickell and Mari Ann Bukovac; Janette Cobb; Patrick and Bonnie Skutch; Dan and Nina Kugler; Pete Ackley; Kristen Debold-Walker; the members of The Clock People GISHWHES Team; Kyra Millar; Melissa Morris; Hollie Smurthwaite and Randy Nichols; Eric Giandelone; George Weber, who was one of the first people to believe in me as a writer, and I haven't forgotten; John Chaplain; Annie "Kimora" Abellana, who keeps me looking fabulous; Marcie Goldbloom; Pat Ruch; DoriAnn Basaraba; Janet Aminoff; Maggy Fouche; Kathleen Weaver; Jonas Apelquist; Lisa Courtley-Rekstad; Dona Benkert and all my classmates in my Advanced Mountain Dulcimer Techniques class at the Old Town School of Folk Music. There are so many others—people who sent kind words, prayers, and even little anonymous gifts. Thank you for your support, and I hope to pay your kindness forward.

I have been blessed with two ball pythons, three chinchillas, four greyhounds, and one lurcher in my life: Monty, Monty II, Rollo, Machu and Picchu, Cleo, Anubis, Giza, Horus, and Lexi. Whether they are with me still or enjoying an endless treat buffet in Pet Heaven, they are always in my heart.

I want to take a moment to remember friends and loved ones no longer with us, many of whom also struggled with cancer: My dad, Norman; Richard and Carl Steiger; Gladys and Adolph Steiger; Mary Clingan; Richard and Susan Macchia; Deborah Huber; George and Michael Zezule; Roberta "Bobbie" Allison; Karen Coleman; Charlene DeBold; May Aldrin; Robert Bjorvik; Diane

Burnside; Theresa, Michael, and Jennifer Butler; Paul Callaway; Nahren Cama; Emily Domasica; Tori Dresbaugh; Cindy Gomez; Kathy Heslinga; J. Edward Johnston; Amy Kleckner; Kevin Maldonado; Adrienne Matzen; Terri Mazza; Barbara Romano; John Salyers; Tina, Tommy, and Mary Ann Wilcox; Raymond Wlodkowski; and Yvonne Zipter.

David Sedaris once gave me special "author shampoo" after a reading to help me with my literary career. It worked well, but it may very well have been carcinogenic. Still I owe him a debt of gratitude for being so kind at a late hour to an aspiring writer.

I would not be the poet or human being I am without the creative influence of the members of Monty Python. Special thanks to Eric Idle for teaching me to always look on the bright side of life and survive cancer in style.

My husband, Matt, took excellent care of me during my ordeal, and I love him now more than ever, so this collection is dedicated to him. The perfect team! < >

Contents

A Quick Fix	15
Cotton Candy, 1983	17
A Bit of a Meltdown	19
Oceanic	20
bean sí	22
Bad News Sonnet	23
The First of the Plagues	24
Encounter with a Possum on an Evening Walk	27
First, the Rules	28
Tarot Reading	30
Toxicity	31
Mizpah	33
Stasis	35
The Olympian Flu	36
Mastectomy	37
Abandonment	38
But Seriously, How Are You Feeling?	39
Tumbling	40
Black Hole, Zoomed Out	41
Follow Up	42
Cerebellum	43
My Ongoing Dispute with My Long-Term Disability Carrier	46
Luna	48
Stage II Procyon lotor	50
The Eternal	52
Level and Plumb	54
Luster	55

A Quick Fix

I remember that I had been really stressed out,
working a lot of nights and weekends,
just a really hectic, crazy time in my life
that lasted about eighteen years.
And, sure, I had gained some weight
and needed blood pressure medications
that were difficult to pronounce
and propped myself up on caffeine,
but none of that seemed particularly serious
until the day my left breast just fell off,
fell right off, hit the floor, and rolled under the couch.

There's about ten years of dust and dog hair under there,
and it was stressful to have my breast just out of reach.
Like when you misplace your eyeglasses
and crawl blindly on your hands and knees,
feeling for the plastic frames on the floor.

Once I found it, I took it with me to Home Depot,
asked an employee in an orange apron for advice.
A female employee, who might understand.
Or maybe she might think I'm an idiot
for losing it in the first place.
But she made some suggestions:
duct tape in Aisle 13,
a glue gun by the Halloween crafts,
hammer and nails in Aisle 42.
I looked uncertain, insecure.
I'd never done this sort of thing before.
"Home Depot will reattach it for you," she suggested.
"It's not that expensive.
Or we've got some breasts you can rent."

I bought a roll of silver duct tape,
just as a quick, temporary fix
and wrapped the tape several times
around my midsection,
keeping it tight,
holding my breast in place,
but of course it's not quite right.
I'm looking for a professional installer,
one who's not too expensive
and has decent reviews on Yelp.

Cotton Candy, 1983

Get sugar drunk as you
inhale the princess pink,
the crayon butterfly blue,
the unicorn mane lilac.
The church volunteer
swirls the white paper cone
around and around
the brim of the silver pan
into the cobwebs of floss
and hands the oversized puff to you,
smiling at your widened eyes.
It's bigger than your head
and your dentist's nightmare.
Your mother will take a bite—
just one—
the rest belongs all to you.

Tear off a piece,
stuff it in your salivating mouth.
It melts,
then goes hard on your tongue,
then vanishes.

It is clutching a sandcastle,
biting into a fluffy cloud.
It is that part of your childhood
where snorting, neighing carousel horses
are alive, with names and individual personalities,
where Tilt-a-Whirls spin cherry red and blurry
on a round blue platform,
where you are at the mercy of the Scrambler,

sliding into your older brother
at the end of the dingy silver car with a squeal,
where you ride a little yellow fire engine with a ringing bell
or a little green car with a honking horn,
waving at your mother each time you pass her by,
and she waves back every time,
before you're too old for those baby rides,
before you have to go meet your friends,
before you follow some boy around,
all moon-faced and dorky,
before you get roped into volunteering in some hot booth,
before you go away for college,
before you are old enough for the beer garden,
before there's really no reason to go back.
It goes so fast,
the cotton candy, that is.
The paper cone wilting in the palm of your sweaty hand,
tiny fingers sticky
and your tongue painted rainbow.

A Bit of a Meltdown

I casually disemboweled myself the other day
in front of a crowd of people.
They gaped at me as my intestines spilled out
onto the dirty, gravelly pavement,
but no one did anything about it.
In the moment, it felt really good,
like something I had been waiting to do for a long time.
And these people deserved to see my evisceration,
the long red and pink ribbons of my entrails
like an overly stretched out Slinky.
Afterwards, I felt quite embarrassed.
It's not really normal behavior.
Messy. Hard to put everything back
where it had been before.
People are going to talk about it,
ask me if I'm okay.
Do I *look* like I'm okay?
This is my colon, right here in my hands.
Do I need to apologize for being unprofessional?
You're not supposed to try to stuff everything back in.
Instead, wrap the organs in a sterile gauze
and calmly walk yourself to the hospital.

Oceanic

Such a surprise
to fall overboard
into the briny sea.
The shock of the cold,
a mouth full of salt,
spitting, coughing.
The waves carelessly tossing you,
batting you back and forth,
like a ball stolen from a smaller kid.
"What's wrong? You want your ball back?
Here it is . . . just catch it!"
The ball is thrown agonizingly high overhead,
straight into the hands of a second bully.
And so it goes,
over and over again,
'til you go home crying,
and your dad says,
you need to stand up for yourself.
There is no alone
more alone
than bobbing in the middle of the sea,
a hundred miles or more from land,
no ships on the horizon,
no desert isles with sandy beaches
palm trees laden with green coconuts,
just the sea and you,
and yes, I know there are millions
of living creatures
swimming beside you, below you,
tickling your feet,
maybe trying to take a bite.

Still, there is no alone more alone.
And the sun beats down,
burning your scalp bright red,
and you have a headache,
and you're burning with thirst,
surrounded by endless water
that you can't drink,
and you think,
This just really sucks.
You wonder if anyone noticed
that you were gone.
Has that cruise ship
continued to cut effortlessly
through the sea
to the next port of call?
Are people still sipping mojitos by the pool,
taking yoga classes on the deck at dawn,
feeling indecisive in front of a large buffet,
bravely walking up to the mic
on karaoke night
after three stiff drinks?
You're going to be shark food soon,
and that's just the way of things here.
Some fish eat,
and some fish get eaten,
and why did you think you were so special?

bean sí

What makes a woman a howling banshee?
The one you hear through
your bedroom's locked window at midnight.
The tall woman,
her body wasted by grief,
gray cloak hanging limply on her slumped shoulders,
her green dress, once a rich velvet,
now covered in wispy silver cobwebs,
her dark eyes sunken and red with tears,
her pale skin a stranger to sunlight,
her red curly hair unwashed and tangled,
her thin lips just the entrance to a jagged cave
from which emerge guttural moans and shrieks.
You look outside and see her silhouette standing
dark and lonely on the hilltop,
battered by the wind.
Her cries are heartbreaking but terrifying too
because it's not herself that she wails for,
but for you.

Bad News Sonnet

I wonder if you could go back in time,
if you had the power to choose,
that day when you were at your prime,
would you have opted to hear the terrible news?

Or would you remain blissfully unaware,
your head a foot deep in the sand,
that life is inherently unfair,
nature never guided by a gentle hand?

Wouldn't you agree
that the worst thing is to have no power,
that the door has no golden key,
that there is no bridge leading to the bright tower,

and you have no choice but to accept it?
There's really nothing I can do? Well, shit.

The First of the Plagues

Really, anything can happen
in Chicago in April:
Pouring rain, thunder and hail
or freak three-foot snowstorms
or sunshine and blue skies
dotted with feathery white clouds.
But we weren't expecting
all those goddamn exploding frogs.

It was a Wednesday morning,
otherwise unremarkable,
warm enough to wear
a lighter jacket.
Skies threatening rain,
but rain wasn't in the forecast.
Also not in the forecast . . .
thousands upon thousands of
small green-gray frogs
covering every surface outside.
Your porch, the sidewalk,
the black asphalt of your driveway,
the hood and trunk and roof of your car.

I had stepped on a couple accidentally
and felt bad about that.
One leaped onto the arm of my jacket,
blinked at me apathetically,
then croaked and jumped away.
Then, maybe a few minutes later,
one by one, the frogs exploded.
Is "exploded" the right word?
No one knows.

But there was a sound like a popping balloon,
then all that remained were some pink guts
splattered on your coat or your car,
against the brick or vinyl siding of your home.
You could hear police sirens and screams.
Frogs bursting all over the city.
Some idiots tried shooting at them
and hit their neighbors instead.
Schools were on lockdown.
Drivers were blinded when pink entrails
covered their windshields,
so cars were careening onto the curb,
colliding with fire hydrants
or smashing into each other.
Hospitals were filled with the victims
of those kinds of accidents
but also patients with panic attacks,
chest pains, and breathing difficulties.

It was a one-time mass amphibian explosion.
By lunchtime or so, it was all over.
In the days that followed,
biologists and ecologists and priests
appeared on morning talk shows
to attempt to explain what had happened.
Some of them tried to characterize the croaking eruption
as a natural self-defense mechanism gone wrong
or some kind of aberrant genetic mutation.
Some of them blamed global warming.
There was talk of bioterrorism
and sinister government conspiracies.
Others called it a pestilence from God.

All I know is,
every dog in the city
thought it was the single best day
of their entire lives.

Encounter with a Possum on an Evening Walk

Beneath the moon I saw
the long naked tail of a possum.
It turned to me,
bared the teeth lining its pointed gray snout,
and loudly hissed
before disappearing into the nearest evergreen shrub.
My dogs barked,
short, panting breaths,
hearts racing, pulling,
ready to give chase, but I held them back,
tightening my grip on their black nylon leashes,
goosebumps dotting my arms.
One dog strained with all her might
towards the bush
where the possum had last been seen.
The other idiotically wrapped his leash
around my legs.
I cursed at them and tried to untangle myself.
I sighed and looked up at Mars,
unusually bright in the sky that night.
I was not in control,
not in control of anything at all.

First, the Rules

Lie here.
Turn on your side.
Stay on your back.
Lie on your stomach.
Most importantly, don't move.
We'll tell you when to breathe.
You'll feel a little poke.
Close your fist.
Open your fist.
Sit in this chair.
Would you like a blanket?
Wait here.
Watch the drip, drip, drip.
Come back for a shot tomorrow.
Take a nap.
But not too many naps.
Don't forget to exercise!
Eat this.
Take this supplement.
Did I tell you how my sister-in-law
went vegan after she was diagnosed?
She didn't even lose her hair.
My aunt died of this,
such horrible suffering.
Be brave!
Avoid this chemical.
It's in everything you eat, drink, and wear.
Have you tried the keto diet?

I've got some essential oils for you.
Read this book.
Join this group.
Buy this lotion.
You've got this!

Tarot Reading

In a Northwest Indiana bedroom,
three girls are bent over the deck of cards,
bought that evening from Barnes & Noble,
the prettiest deck they had,
with soft female nudes,
vibrant colors,
shiny gold edges.
the cards shuffled
and arranged in the shape of a cross.
The girls are laboriously looking up
and reading the meaning of each card aloud,
The Magician, The Chariot, The Four of Staves,
The Five of Cups reversed . . .
The ancient power of sight and prognostication
being harnessed on this night
to lay bare the mind
of an oblivious teenage boy.

Toxicity

Thirty-five years ago today,
government agents appeared
in the town of Daffodil Hill
with their white hazmat suits
and their clicking, beeping instruments,
and they declared the town and its environs
to be "toxic to humans and animals,"
thanks to the local pesticide manufacturing company
located at the edge of town.
Cockroaches and centipedes having the last laugh
as the governor ordered a mandatory evacuation.
Angry letters
Protests
Screaming voices echoing in a municipal building
Lost jobs
Crashing property values
Sunk cost
Empty bleachers in the high school gym
No more Daffodil Hill Hornbills in black and gold.
A circle of juniors singing the fight song,
long-haired girls sobbing.
Like, who cares that much about their high school?
But maybe you would,
if it were forced to be closed,
all your friends and teachers scattered across the state,
your dad with a new job,
in a new town,
and the kids there make fun of you for being
from the toxic waste dump,
and you're one of the lucky ones.
The state bought people's homes
at rock-bottom prices.

Nature reclaimed the strip mall on Park Street.
Only one man refused to leave and lives there still,
68-year-old Jerry McCarthy,
angry, drunken, cussing.
He pulled a shotgun on the trooper who knocked on his door
with the evacuation notice.
The whole ghost town is his domain now,
king of empty houses and stores.
He collects bits of debris from Daffodil Hill
and arranges it on his front lawn.
It all looks as trashy as he is,
but it doesn't matter.
He says he's going to run a museum one day,
a museum of Daffodil Hill,
and he'll tell his visitors what happened here,
how there was a town here,
not a great town,
but a nice one,
and all that's been erased now,
as though anyone would want to visit such a monument,
risking birth defects and certain rare cancers,
while walking on the poisoned ground.

Mizpah

Just my dumb luck
for loving an astronaut.
An unfortunate accident,
I was told.
He took a wrong turn into a black hole.
They didn't want to get into details
about what happened to him there, but I know.
Spaghettification,
which sounds hilarious
until it's happening to you.
I don't mean to be glib.
It's the most awful thing
I can think of.
But because of the weird things that happen
with space and time
when you go through a black hole,
I keep getting phone calls from him.
Phone calls from before his death,
just about every day now.
I try to warn him about what has happened,
in my past and his future,
but nothing has changed in the present,
so I don't think fate is mutable.
But we just have some nice conversations now.
He asks me about my day,
and I ask him what he's seen.
The cool blue of an ice planet,
its lumpy grey rock of a moon.
Gassy clouds of violet, red, and orange.
Tiny yellow and blue dots in this endless black field;

they are whole galaxies that he will never reach.
I tell him about the rosebush in the backyard,
the one he planted and I neglect.
The fuchsia blossoms and tender green leaves
turn brown, curl up, and fall off in the fall,
but they always return.

Stasis

Tardigrade,
water bear,
moss piglet.
Tiny little hands and feet
on microscopic limbs,
searching for algae
to suck up with its vacuum mouth
into its translucent body.
When the world ends,
it curls up in a ball,
unknowing but
impenetrable,
indestructible.
I don't know what it dreams of,
but it awakes unfazed
by the ice storms and the drought
and the emptiness of space.
Just like quarantine naps
on a stained microsuede couch.
The empty can of pizza-flavored Pringles
lies on its side on the floor,
just out of my reach.
I draw my knees up,
put my glasses up for safety.
Isolated,
uncontaminated.
Wake me up when this is over.

The Olympian Flu

Pan was the cause
of the divine pandemic.
Zeus, that creepy old rapist,
finally fell dead off his Olympian throne,
and all the virgins of Greece cheered.
Hera caught the bug from Zeus
and passed it on to Aphrodite.
Aphrodite gave it to her son, Eros,
and he caused an outbreak
with his infected arrows.
Athena took to her bed
and napped for a thousand years.
Dionysius merely complained of a light cough
and drank wine sweetened with honey.
Meanwhile on Earth,
wars raged without divine protection,
the future could not be foretold,
and a young man,
who had been in love with a magical silver fawn,
wandered lonely through the woods,
wondering where she had gone.

Mastectomy

I never thought I'd be the kind of person
who would have my own plastic surgeon.
I don't even wear eyeliner.
Nevertheless, I have a plastic surgeon,
and he seems proud of the previous day's work.

I'm sure he sees these freshly deflated tits
all the time, but it's still a shock to me.
My left breast looks like it was in
a farming accident.
"Ol' Lefty has never been the same
since she got caught up in the thresher."
Or maybe it had been run over by a truck,
and then the truck backed up
and ran over it again.
It's now covered in off-putting shades
of sickly yellow and angry purple,
misshapen and concave in places.
Like the roadkill possum
that's not quite dead yet,
hissing and spitting and cursing at you
as it crawls across the road.

It will get better, I guess.
You'll see me soon
in some black Nine Inch Nails t-shirt,
covered in dog hair,
and probably a dollop of mustard
(you know me),
and you would never know
this happened to me.

Abandonment

I saw something funny online the other day,
so I texted it to you and waited.
Most days, I think you tune me out,
like one might choose to ignore
a yapping chihuahua bouncing on his two hind legs
to see through the bottom of a screen door.
Reason and common sense would tell me to surrender,
give you up to the distance that separates us both now,
but then sometimes you reply, "ha ha."
So I continue to send out these radio signals
from my distant planet,
cartoonishly large headphones pressed to my ears,
as I close my eyes and listen for any type of beeps or blips
across galaxies of hissing static.

If I were in prison in a foreign country,
sitting on a cold metal bench in a dark cell,
where I don't speak the language
and where one can bribe the guards,
except I don't have money,
I would most want to talk to you in that moment.
I'd beg the guard for a single phone call.
That's not something that's guaranteed in that country,
let me tell you.
And with a heavy sigh of annoyance, he'd agree,
because I would be so loud and insistent,
and I'd have to talk on some ancient black rotary phone
attached to the cement block wall.
I'd call your number,
even though I know it would go straight to voicemail.

But Seriously, How Are You Feeling?

It was
arson pain
gunshot pain
firework pain
bridge collapsing pain
World War One trench pain
cave diver suffering from the bends pain
astronaut on a spacewalk cut from his tether, floating into space,
silently screaming pain.
But now it just really itches.

Tumbling

I've been falling in my dreams lately.
I don't know what the context is.
I'm just plummeting, the world a blur,
my stomach somewhere in my throat.
Nothing to grab at to slow my descent.
And I really feel it,
I really feel myself falling,
so I call out in a panic,
"helphelphelphelphelphelp!"
And my husband gets annoyed,
because I've just woken him up
and terrified him with my cries,
but I'm actually fine,
lying on my back on the couch.
And when I am about to crash land,
my eyes flutter open,
but I don't feel safe,
not for the rest of the day.

Black Hole, Zoomed Out

A child god scribbles orange and yellow
against an infinite black background,
the crayon's tip breaking under the pressure.
The feverish scrawl turns into a jellyfish,
energetic, hungry, greedy, short-tempered,
with one long tentacle outstretched
to suck everything up into itself,
sweeping all matter and light into
its lurid, fiery, golden center.

Follow Up

Rip off the tape,
peel away the bandages,
snip the stitches,
remove the bloody drains.
Ignore the yelps of pain,
the wincing eyes.
Look critically at your work.
Not the prettiest embroidery
on a flawed sallow canvas.

Cerebellum

Kyle sneezed particularly hard one day,
and the gray matter of his brain
slid easily out of his right ear
and glopped onto the white tile
of the kitchen floor.
This surprised his fiancée, Kristin.
A second earlier, she had been dictating
the seating chart for their wedding;
the next moment
Kyle's entire mind absconded.
"Pick it up!" she cried,
but Kyle merely stared into the distance,
his lower jaw hanging open a bit.
Finally Kristin had the presence of mind
to call 911, but the dispatcher didn't understand,
and the paramedics were astounded.
Kyle's body was not only still alive,
but his brain had started scooting
around on the floor
making little squeaking noises
and leaving a trail of clear fluid behind it.
The paramedics were afraid to touch it,
so eventually Kristin,
who always wound up having to do everything herself,
scooped it up and put it in a cardboard box.
Kyle's body seemed fine,
could walk on its own,
as long as you led it by the hand.
His body on a stretcher,
and his mind in a box,
Kyle was transported to the hospital,

and a team of neurologists stared at him
for a good long while.
Kyle's mind was electric and active
in a clear plastic incubator next to his body,
and his heart kept on beating,
and his organs kept on organing,
but Kristin was fairly sure the wedding
would have to be postponed at the very least,
deposits lost,
gifts returned.
Meanwhile, Kyle's body grew more independent,
could change the channel on the TV,
could operate a laptop,
could continue working on a part-time basis,
and even leave comments on Twitter.
His body was eventually discharged from the hospital,
since doctors weren't sure what else to do with it.
They planned to keep his brain for research purposes.
Kristin decided the wedding could go on after all.
I mean, she had the dress and everything.
The night before the nuptials,
Kyle's body snuck into the hospital
to free his brain.
His arms carefully cradled it,
Jello-like gray matter.
It trembled and whimpered a little
during this reunion.
Kyle's body drove his brain to a forest preserve,
and he set it gently in the limbs of an oak tree.
Kyle's brain was never seen again.
The neurologists were devastated.

Kyle and Kristin's wedding went off without a hitch.
A few months later, his body was promoted
to assistant vice president,
and the future never seemed brighter.

My Ongoing Dispute with My Long-Term Disability Carrier

I imagine a man in his mid-thirties,
recently married, just bought a house.
His wife also found out they were pregnant.
Working at his cubicle despite the virus,
beige carpet, beige walls, beige ceiling,
phones ringing, fingers clacking on keyboards.
He's in Tampa, and there's a palm tree just outside
the nearest window,
and it's hot in his cubicle when the sun shines in,
like a greenhouse.
And he's wearing a polo shirt and khakis,
freshly washed, unwrinkled,
and he used to have abs,
when he played beach volleyball a lot,
but now he's softened,
a pale belly to match his wife's,
and his hairline might be starting to recede,
but his wife told him not to worry about it,
he looks fine.
And he just ate the lunch he brought from home,
but he's still hungry,
and it's only 1:30.
And everyone's supposed to be wearing a facemask
in the common areas of the office,
and some people wear double-masks even in their cubicles,
and some don't wear any at all,
just daring you to say something about it.
And he checks his email and checks the news
and checks his fantasy football team,
and another half an hour crawls by,

and finally he gets around to reading my letter,
finding words like "bad faith" and "retaliation" and "civil action,"
and just for a brief moment,
as he rejects my most recent claim,
he wishes I'd drop dead.

Luna

The quadrillionaire,
so rich he actually bought the Moon,
launched into space to survey his purchase.
When he arrived,
he found it was a lonely, grey, dark, empty rock,
devoid of air and life
but still, he thought, it was worth the price,
paid in full to the United Nations,
despite worldwide protest
and angry posts on social media.
He bounced around a bit on the dusty surface
and planted a flag with his corporation's logo
in what he thought was a prominent spot.
He watched the Earth rise,
gigantic and blue,
in front of him and shed a tear.

Then he was bored and ready to go home,
but there was a mechanical problem with his space shuttle.
His pilot frowned at wires and computer chips
and hunks of gleaming metal.
They needed a replacement part,
but due to bureaucracy and budget constraints,
it would take a couple of years to arrive.
The quadrillionaire and his pilot
were well stocked in food and supplies
but didn't have much in common.
He was still making money, at least,
the quadrillionaire, that is.
Because he had the Moon trademarked and copyrighted,
and there was a fee to gaze at it with your lover,

photograph it hanging low and large and orange
over a majestic rock formation in the desert,
describe it in your poem,
teach its phases to bored schoolchildren,
and allow it to influence your tides.
On a clear night, you could try to view
the stranded quadrillionaire with your backyard telescope.
But most people said it wasn't worth
the monthly subscription.

Stage II Procyon lotor

When you have cancer, I wouldn't say it's *just* like
having a large raccoon up in your attic,
but it's not *unlike*
having a large raccoon up in your attic.
Maybe you hear some scratching noises
while you're in the living room watching TV,
and you think, *Hm, that's unusual,*
but then you decide that
it was just the air conditioner turning on,
and you return to your show.
You do this for about three to nine months.
The scratching noise grows more persistent,
accompanied by some loud *bangs* in the night
that are definitely a sign of something amiss,
and you really ought to call someone, so you do.
That person tells you he can show up for an estimate
in about two weeks. (The estimate is not free.)
Finally the wildlife guy arrives,
looks around the exterior of your house,
takes some pictures and some measurements,
and tells you that in about another two weeks,
he'll be able to confirm whether
you have a raccoon in your attic.
I mean, you can't just go rushing up there
and try to catch this thing with your bare hands.
What if there's like eight of them up there?
What if they get into the rest of the house?
You're left there alone with the scratching and the *bangs*
and worry about waking up with it in your bed,
but two weeks pass, and you receive a phone call,
and the wildlife guy is very sorry,
but all signs point to you having a raccoon.

So a month or so goes by,
no end to the scratching and the *bangs,*
Are they having babies up there? Who knows?
But the wildlife guy returns,
goes up into your attic with a trap,
and comes back down triumphant,
a large, angry raccoon in a small wire cage.
Thank God!
But then you see him taking more pictures and measurements
because he can't be sure that there's not any more up there,
and he'll just have to keep checking every three months or so.
So when you hear a slight scratching sound at night,
You just have to wonder if there's a new raccoon
or if previous raccoon residents had just never left,
and your insurance informs you they aren't paying for the damage,
not now, not ever.

The Eternal

in memory of Yvonne Zipter

As I rise,
the intravenous lines and tubes
turn into thin red branches
and sharp green needles,
and I inhale deep their wild perfume.
I rise higher and see my life's path—
the tiny choices branching off the consequential decisions—
separate limbs for the steps I never took
but could have.
Regrets fall gently away,
little brown twigs scattered on the ground.

Formless,
I see more clearly now.
Clusters of leaves,
grey, flaking bark,
everything so quiet here,
compared to the humming and beeping of the monitors
and the droning of the television on the wall
and the muted honks and ambulance sirens
just outside my window.
Now there is only the rustling of a gentle breeze
and the chirping of songbirds
and the outsized clatter of a squirrel nearby but unseen.

Everyone I have ever known,
every place I have ever planned to go,
everything I have ever worried about,
seems so tiny now.
A single blade of verdant grass for every wish I made.
My friends, my family, my loves continue without me.
They go to work, stand in line for coffee,
watch TV, and fall asleep on the couch.
They laugh, they sigh, they cry until they get a headache.

I drink in the golden sunlight
that warms and cheers me,
not knowing how long it's been.
Minutes since I left, or perhaps years.
If you think of me,
worried that you can't remember my voice,
look for me in this quiet place.
I am here, not waiting.
I am at peace.
I am.

Level and Plumb

I want to wake with the dawn,
not finally close my eyes to slumber
with the first rays of the sun.
I want to be healthy,
I want to be clean,
I want to sigh with satisfaction and say,
"I'm done. I finished early."
I want to be extraordinary,
I want to be something greater than I am.
But I am obtuse angles,
the tile floor with one misplaced black square.
I don't tear neatly at the perforation.
I need a nap.
I am the errant lock of hair that sticks straight up defiantly,
the phone screen with a thin but unmistakable crack.
I try every day,
and every day there's something I've left undone.
And every morning,
when I'm finally, officially awake,
I promise that today—this day—will be different,
I will whir and hum like the efficient machine
that replaces the clumsy human workers.

Luster

A few weeks after the end of the world,
everything was bathed in a soft rose gold light,
like an eternal dawn,
and it was quiet, finally quiet
so you could hear the birds chirping
and the crickets singing.
No more fire or smoke, just a gentle breeze
and everything pink, peach, and golden,
the grass growing as high as your hips,
and you touched the tips of the green blades
as you swam through.
And the earth seemed relieved then,
like after a migraine or a fever breaks,
and it felt so good to feel good again.
And at night, it was dark, but not lonely.
The stars and planets and long, bright meteor streaks
decorated the black fabric of space
that hung over the sleeping land.

About the Author

Karen Steiger is a poet, fiction writer, and breast cancer survivor living in Schaumburg, IL, with her beloved husband, Matt, and two dogs, Horus and Lexi. Her work is published in *The Wells Street Journal, Arsenika, Black Bough Poetry, Ang(st), Perhappened, Kaleidotrope, Mineral Lit Mag, Rejection Letters, Versification, Sledgehammer Lit, Bombfire Lit, Lamp Lit,* and others.

www.ingramcontent.com/pod-product-compliance
Lightning Source LLC
Chambersburg PA
CBHW031206160426
43193CB00008B/520